PRAISE

BUY LOW, SELL HIGH, STUPID!

"John's out-of-the-box thinking and the way he looks at the market is a refreshing and unique approach to the 'good old boy' corporate brokerage concepts. This book will give you insight to the past, present, and future markets and how they did, do, and will make you money. Enjoy the book. It's working for me!"

—BRIAN D. LACKEY, DDS, *client*

"Having had mixed success with my own investing, I was elated to discover someone who was genuinely interested, and passionate, about helping us—'the proverbial little guy.' As John explained his disciplined actively managed approach, keeping at least 30 percent in cash, waiting for 'opportunity buying,' I felt we had found the guru that would make us financially better off and, best of all, allow us to sleep at night!

Our instincts were proven correct, as John's complex and 'right-on-the-money' successful strategies netted us over 25 percent, and we started in a correction. His disciplined strategy is the real deal for small investors like me!

—VINNIE PAPA, *client*

"John Scambray is the real deal. He understands invest-ments and market strategies from the ground floor up. He has a knack for realizing the potential for the average investor and is usually right with his investment advice and strategies. I have been fortunate enough to have been on the NYSE podium twice to ring the morning bell. I have yet to know of anyone who has the in-depth knowledge and work ethic to make investments work as John does. This book is a must-read for both beginning investors and seasoned investors. Both will find nuggets that will help them in their financial endeavors."

—ALLEN BENNETT, *client*

No clients were compensated for providing these testimonials.

BUY LOW, SELL HIGH, STUPID!

BUY LOW, SELL HIGH, STUPID!

A SIMPLE, NO BS GUIDE
TO BUILDING AND MANAGING A
SUCCESSFUL INVESTMENT PORTFOLIO

JOHN SCAMBRAY

Published by Advantage, Charleston, South Carolina.
Member of Advantage Media Group.

ADVANTAGE is a registered trademark, and the Advantage colophon is a trademark of Advantage Media Group, Inc.

Printed in the United States of America.

10 9 8 7 6 5 4 3 2 1

ISBN: 978-1-64225-225-5
LCCN: 2021919619

Cover design by Carly Blake.
Layout design by Mary Hamilton.

This publication is designed to provide accurate and authoritative information in regard to the subject matter covered. It is sold with the understanding that the publisher is not engaged in rendering legal, accounting, or other professional services. If legal advice or other expert assistance is required, the services of a competent professional person should be sought.

Advantage Media Group is proud to be a part of the Tree Neutral® program. Tree Neutral offsets the number of trees consumed in the production and printing of this book by taking proactive steps such as planting trees in direct proportion to the number of trees used to print books. To learn more about Tree Neutral, please visit **www.treeneutral.com**.

Advantage Media Group is a publisher of business, self-improvement, and professional development books and online learning. We help entrepreneurs, business leaders, and professionals share their Stories, Passion, and Knowledge to help others Learn & Grow. Do you have a manuscript or book idea that you would like us to consider for publishing? Please visit **advantagefamily.com**.

To my father and best friend, Eugene—
the hardest-working, most generous, ethical,
honest, loving, best man I know.

LEGAL DISCLOSURES/DISCLAIMERS

This opinion material is written by One Source Health & Wealth Management and contains general information to help you understand basic investment strategies.

Throughout the book, we may generally discuss different financial vehicles; however, nothing we say should be construed as a recommendation to buy or sell any financial vehicle, nor should it be used to make decisions today about your investments.

Our goal with this book is to expose you to ideas and financial vehicles that may help you work toward your financial goals. Please understand that we cannot make any promises or guarantees that you will accomplish such goals. All investments are subject to risk, including the potential loss of principal. No investment strategy can guarantee a profit or protect against loss in periods of declining values. Past performance is not a guarantee of future results.

Any references to protection benefits generally refer to insurance products. Insurance and annuity product guarantees are backed by the financial strength and claims-paying ability of the issuing insurance company.

This book is designed to provide general information on the subjects covered. It is not, however, intended to provide specific legal or tax advice and cannot be used to avoid tax penalties or to promote, market, or recommend any tax plan or arrangement. Please note that One Source Health & Wealth Management and its representatives do not give legal or tax advice. You are encouraged to consult your tax advisor or attorney.

Despite efforts to be accurate and current, this book may contain out-of-date information; we are under no obligation to advise you of any subsequent changes related to the topics discussed in this book.

At the end of the book, you will be provided an opportunity to visit with us one-on-one to discuss your specific circumstance in a private, comfortable setting. There is no obligation to you for this visit. At this visit you may be provided with information regarding the purchase of investment products or establishing an advisory relationship.

CONTENTS

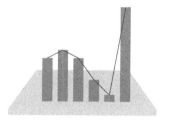

ABOUT THE AUTHOR

J ohn began his career more than twenty-five years ago as a financial services representative, helping uniquely successful individuals, businesses, and families make crucial financial decisions with confidence. John has led advisory and wealth management business units and has spent almost three decades honing his portfolio management, financial planning, and risk reduction knowledge in his effort to add value to his clients' financial lives. John is extremely passionate about creating investment portfolios that exceed his clients' expectations. He constantly strives to learn and improve his knowledge of high finance, most importantly keeping current with winning strategies that yield above-average results. He is a certified portfolio manager and fiduciary who puts his clients' interests first. When John is not hard at work for his clients, he loves spending time with his wife of twenty-five years, visiting his three grown daughters, and playing with the family's Bernese mountain dog, Sophie.

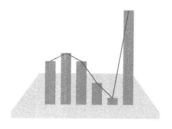

ACKNOWLEDGMENTS

I could not have written this book without the support and friendship of my two primary partners, Chad Frazier and Doug Emitte. A big thanks must be written here, too, to my partner and friend Ed Outland, who has made talking about our business fun again, especially after teaching me about using talk radio to get the word out. To our support rock, Kathy, who does the mundane day-to-day tasks for us, which allowed me to take the time to write my thoughts down in this book—thank you. To my cousins, Billy and Scott. Billy, you are more than a cousin; you are my brother. Thank you for your relentless competitiveness and incredible sense of humor; keep fighting for what you deserve. Scott, the sports almanac in the family, you gave me someone to look up to; thank you and congratulations on an incredible career in education. Our students and their parents owe you big time for your service to the community. Thank you to my kids, Madison, Jessica, and Katie, whom I love more than my own life; my mother, Carolyn (whom I get my wonderful personality from); my dad, Eugene; my incredible and beautiful big sister, Dina; and all our family and friends, like my best friend Jason, who put up with me and my ranting about everything. Finally, I must thank and acknowledge the most important person in my life who has stuck by me through thick and thin, through good times and bad, my beautiful wife, Stacey—thank you, honey. I love you.

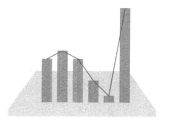

WHY WORK WITH ME?

How does an average guy ultimately become responsible for helping people make millions of dollars over the last several decades? What made him change his mind so completely about the kind of work he had been doing for big financial institutions for so many years? Why did he buck the status quo? Why would he want to give up on leading large investment programs to help individuals with their finances directly?

Read on to find out.

I had what people would call a "normal" childhood. I grew up in a normal middle-class family of four with two dogs, living in a four-bedroom house with a two-car garage in a neighborhood filled with kids playing in the streets until it was time to come in for dinner. After a great childhood and adventurous college experiences, I eventually found my calling: selling investments. I tried a few different things along the way, but helping people achieve their investment goals became my passion—and it still is today.

It really began for me in the late 1990s. I was working at a major national Wall Street brokerage house where I was often told what I could and could not do for clients, such as: "Here's what you can recommend," "Here are the companies that we think you should follow," "Here's the list of mutual funds and insurance products you can recommend," and "Here's the list of stocks that our firm recommends you only solicit." I never liked being told what to do, and I was always skeptical when told what specific products or stocks I could sell. I never felt right about it, and I always wanted to know what else was out there in the big world that could make my clients a lot of money.

Then, it happened. I found out I had the ability to think outside the box, which was often the opposite of what I was being told to do. When the analysts at the firm I was working for downgraded PG&E, a large Northern California power company, to "sell" because it was going through self-imposed financial hardship and potential bankruptcy, everyone I knew in the investment business was saying, "Stay away, PG&E is a terrible investment." I thought, *How can that be?* At that time, and still to this day, there really was no other option for energy in most parts of Northern California for most people. I was on PG&E; everybody I knew was on PG&E.

I started looking into the company's stock and decided that, yes, if you bought the stock, the growth on your PG&E stock might be iffy for a while. However, PG&E's twenty-five-dollar preferred securities could be bought at a huge discount for around sixteen dollars per share. Since those securities performed like a bond with an 8 percent coupon or interest rate attached, that meant what could be bought for around sixteen dollars would pay twenty-five dollars when matured, plus the 8 percent interest. If PG&E went out of business, an investor would lose money. But I thought, *If PG&E is the only option around, how can it go out of business?* It was too big to fail, and I knew others would agree. I decided to call people up, introduce myself, and ask one key question: "Do you pay your PG&E bill on time?" I figured one of three things would happen: (1) they would hang up, (2) they would ask why I wanted to know, or (3) they would answer, "Yes, I do." If they answered number three, I knew I was potentially talking to a new client.

In fact, that year, I brought in more new accounts than anyone in our entire office and was third in the company nationwide. And I did it by doing the opposite of what everyone else was saying to do, which was not the status quo. And those shares? Not only did those PG&E preferred shares go back to twenty-five dollars, they then started selling at a premium, and we cashed out for insane profits for my clients.

That was just one of the early linchpins that began to shape my investment management while working for big financial services firms. Early on I saw how large firms and big banks don't trust or let their financial advisors think for themselves and their clients. I saw how these firms would take advantage of their average investors by not giving them the same advice and value as large investors. I saw how somebody with millions of dollars received access, guidance, expertise, service, and value that's different from somebody without millions of dollars.

When I worked for big financial institutions, they expected great results primarily for their firm, their executives, their shareholders, and then their clients last. Today, when I hear a big firm say they want the best results for their clients, I have to laugh. If that's true, why do large financial firms, especially banks, make billions of dollars in profit every year and pay huge bonuses to their executives, but then pay virtually nothing in interest to their customers, plus cut their dividends on their stock? It's to achieve their plan targets on their earnings per share and return on equity so that they can pay off their key shareholders and corporate officers off the backs of their bread-and-butter customers. It reminds me of a line I heard in an old famous stockbroker movie when referring to a bank: "They're so conservative, they don't pay any interest at all!"

Today, I still don't believe that major financial corporations, especially large banks, have their clients' best interests at heart. At my firm, we make more money if you make more money —I'm jumping ahead a bit, but I couldn't resist sharing that point. While I was working for a large bank with an investment division, I was responsible for billions of dollars and tens of millions of dollars in revenue and profits. I got to that level of financial responsibility because of my competitiveness, desire to win, wanting more out of life, and not being satisfied with the status quo. From what I've seen, there is nothing more *not in your best interest* than what a bank will do for you, its core customer, financially. When a potential client tells me what the bank is paying them in interest on their accounts, and what they accept as a good rate of return, I try not to laugh. I do everything in my power that my decades of experience have taught me to show my potential client why they should not put more than two to three months of living expenses in a bank. I don't want my clients to settle for less than what they deserve and to certainly not settle for what the mainstream banks pay their core customer.

> **AT MY FIRM, WE MAKE MORE MONEY IF YOU MAKE MORE MONEY.**

Unfortunately, whether it's banks, national brokerage houses, or any type of big financial organization, they reserve only the best people, best investment solutions, and best interest rates for their biggest, most profitable clients.

It's now my passion and career goal to bring more creative investment solutions to people with less than millions of dollars, creative investment solutions that most investors will never have access to because they do not have the amount of investable dollars required at most large investment firms. Since 2015, I've been helping through my own investment advisory firm, which I started with a few long-term colleagues. We thought: *Why can't we show people—average investors—retirees and preretirees, how to make money the way that people make with larger account balances? Why can't we deliver to average investors the same kinds of custom and complex strategies that people with those larger amounts of capital have access to?*

Today, that's what we do for primarily baby boomers with investable assets of $250,000 or more and small- to medium-sized company retirement plans. We work with people who every day want to know: "How do I minimize risk, boost returns, and warrant a more active money-management style?" "How do I employ something that's only reserved for the wealthy to make money in a market going up or down?" "How do I protect my money?"

In the chapters ahead, I'm going to share with you the difference between financial advisors and portfolio managers, why buy-and-hold is for suckers, tips about financial planning, how fear and greed drive emotional investing, and why Wall Street is not your friend. I'll also share why you don't have to be wealthy to make money on your money, some strategies to beat the status quo, what it means to be fair and transparent, and how to get started, including my disciplined asset allocation approach.

Case in point, when a client tells me they did what they were taught and the results were "pretty good," it sounds like an oxymoron to me. Pretty good. To me that means it's just okay. If it's pretty good, it's less than good. I want great for you and our clients. And I'm not talking about unrealistic expectations, but I am talking about expecting more. If you want great too, then you need to be with somebody who doesn't settle for pretty good.

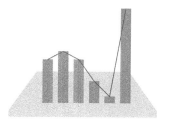

CHAPTER ONE

IS THIS YOU?

W hen it comes to wealth and investment management, I want you to become *excited* about being a more involved and more active investor, *educated* in the different options available to you, and *empowered* by the realization that you are finally on the right track to smarter, less volatile, and more confident investing.

That's what we did for our client Joe, who had been listening to our radio show, "The Wise Money Guys," for some time before he finally decided to pick up the phone and call. He wanted to talk about his portfolio, which at the time was with a well-known national investment brokerage company. He had always liked his financial advisor there, but by the time he sat down with me, his $1.5 million portfolio had dropped to $1.2 million. Why? He didn't know why.

Joe, who was eighty-nine years old, had ridden out a few market ups and downs. But this time was different. He was down $300,000, and his advisor had never called. In fact, it was Joe who picked up the phone and asked his advisor, "My account keeps going down. Should we do anything different?" The advisor just replied, "No, just stay the course, and you'll be fine," which is the typical answer.

Is that true? Is "stay the course" a good strategy when there is a large market decline? History suggests that, eventually, if you stay the course, you may be fine. But here's the deal: Joe was eighty-nine years old. How long should he be expected to "stay the course" and wait for the overall stock market and his account to go back up?

I looked at his portfolio, and, as I suspected, the reason for the major decline was that Joe was not invested properly in the right strategies for his life goals or his age. In fact, there really wasn't a "strategy" to his portfolio at all, except to keep buying the same asset stock mutual funds through dividend and capital gain reinvestment. In other words, his $1.5 million was entirely in a long-term growth strategy that was subject to market ups and downs that happened in the same proportion with the ups and downs of the stock market, known as a "beta of 1." Everything in his portfolio was perfectly correlated, and there were no hedges or defensive and neutral investment positions of any kind. Why would anyone think that a 100 percent all stock with a near perfect correlation to the S&P 500 was a good investment model for Joe? Any idea? You could probably guess what my ideas and thoughts were about his investment portfolio already.

Once we moved his account over and drastically restructured and rebuilt his portfolio, within four months, Joe's portfolio balance was more than $1.4 million and was on a much sounder investment path and potential return to profitability. By the way, it's been approximately a year and a half, and Joe's account is over $1,625,000. Do you think Joe is happier, especially since he has less stock market risk than he did before? Of course he is.

YOU DECIDE...

- "Stay the course" is often not the best investment strategy.

- Meet with a portfolio manager to see if your investments are properly allocated and match your level of risk.

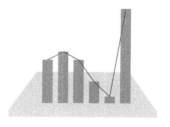

CHAPTER TWO

THE LESS IS MORE "STRATEGY"—NOT!

I often get asked the question by people typically in their sixties up to Joe's age: "How do I live in retirement on less money?" My answer: Why should you live in retirement on less money? Who gave you that "strategy?" You didn't work the majority of your adult life to have less than what you began with, say thirty years ago.

Yet that's what the media, banks, advisors, mutual fund companies, and, worst of all, financial planners all pound into you. That you should be satisfied with a lower station in life during your retirement and golden years. A financial advisor or planner would never tell a person with $5 million: "You should be satisfied with less of a life in retirement." Why should someone with less than $5 million be satisfied with less than the life they are used to in retirement? Ultimately, it's important to have little to no debt in retirement, but

11

you should want more or at least want the same income and way of life in your retirement that you are accustomed to.

WHY SHOULD YOU, WITH YOUR HARD-EARNED DOLLARS, ACCEPT THE STATUS QUO?

As I mentioned in the introduction, people with more money have access to a different level of investment strategies and solutions at most major advisory firms—but it doesn't have to be that way. Why should you, with your hard-earned dollars, accept the status quo? Just what is that status quo? Let's look at just a few of the basic types of investments that most people have that make them believe they should "just accept less."

CHECKING, SAVINGS, MONEY MARKET, CERTIFICATE OF DEPOSIT

Most people put the majority of their savings, not just their emergency reserves, in a bank; typically, in a big bank that pays very little to no interest on a checking or savings account. Bank investments may also include a money market account or a CD for which you may earn a little more interest but still next to nothing. But whether it's a savings account, checking account, money market, or CD, it all adds up to one thing: the big banks making billions of dollars in profit each year and paying you virtually nothing in interest.

It's a harsh but accepted truth that big banks make big money, and they make that money on the backs of their core customers. The reality is that even if you keep a large amount of money in the bank, they will probably give you a special rate for your high balance.

But guess what? That's going to be 0.50 percent to 1.00 percent. On $1 million, 0.50 percent, that's a dismal $5,000 a year. *Wow. Thank you, Big Bank.* (Thanks for nothing.) At the same time, those banks are turning around and issuing credit cards on which they charge on average 19.99 percent. They make auto loans with your money charging around 5 percent. Mortgages using your money they typically charge 3 to 6 percent. They have investment reserves that earn 5 percent or more. They earn more than that on their real estate holdings. Not to mention the billions they make on income from things like the discount fees on credit card transactions and more fees such as nonsufficient funds charges of thirty dollars per returned item, monthly account service charges, and on and on and on. They are making billions of dollars in revenue and profits with your money and paying you nothing for the privilege of being their disposable customer.

Do you need a bank checking or savings for your day-to-day expenses? Absolutely. But should you keep anything above what you need on a day-to-day basis for two to three months in there? No, because by doing so you're giving money away. You're letting that bank use your money and pay you virtually nothing for it. Whether it's a savings account, checking account, money market, or CD, it all adds up to the bank using your money to make billions while you make little to no return.

It's hard for me to fathom that so many people often keep most if not all of their liquid investable money in the bank because they worry about liquidity, being able to access their investments when needed. Nowadays, you can get to virtually anything very quickly. Everything is electronic. Everything is transferable (anything that we do for you is transferable). Investment accounts are linked to your checking accounts so you can move money with just a few clicks. So why would you keep your money, beyond your immediate financial needs, inside of a bank that pays you nothing? Wouldn't you like to know better ways for your money to make you money? Let's talk about something that is ironic to me and should be to you too.

CORPORATE BONDS

Many of our clients have bonds that pay about 3 percent and mature in five years or more. But most people don't buy corporate bonds, especially their bank's bonds, which may be available on the secondary or primary market (newly issued debt). Here again, when it comes to their bank, people are concerned about liquidity and safety, and they are willing to forgo making a decent interest rate on their money in these volatile times, so they invest in a typical account that pays from 0.05 percent to 0.50 percent (savings, checking, money markets, CDs). Yet the risk for buying corporate bank bonds versus putting the money into a bank account is ironically the same. Oh, I know what you are going to say if you are one of those people who think the FDIC is the be-all and end-all, and that's okay. But stay with me here. The only way you don't get paid on your corporate bank bond is if that bank goes out of business; herein lies the irony. Nobody puts their money in a bank account—even with the knowledge of the FDIC—because they believe the bank might go out of business. So if you trust a big bank to pay you back when your one- to five-year CD matures, why not trust a bank to pay you back when your bond matures? Hmmm. For you more advanced investors reading this, if you are holding your bond to maturity, interest rate risk doesn't matter. This is one of those deep instilled beliefs by many that it is okay to be paid virtually no interest by your bank for the privilege of FDIC coverage and no volatility on your bank accounts. It's just silly.

OPEN-ENDED MUTUAL FUNDS

Another basic investment that the majority of the investing public own is open-ended mutual funds. I'll try not to bore you with them, but we must chat about them just a bit because this is what the majority of the investing public is sold each and every day. Some of the things I don't like about funds of this type are that neither you nor I have control over what is owned in the mutual fund, nor do you have control over the daily inflows and outflows of new or departing money. Also, open-ended mutual funds only price once per day; they do not trade in real time. Yet they are highly marketed as the investment of choice for most people, especially in their employer retirement plan, even though their potentially high expenses drag down your retirement's performance. Also, transactions, whether a purchase or liquidation, take two days to settle in your portfolio, and that can limit your ability to time your investment changes in some cases. I know, you have learned that time in the market is more important than timing the market, and I agree, for the most part.

Most people own mutual funds in their IRA or their company retirement plan, like a 401(k). Sometimes that looks good. You feel like you're doing a good thing. You're putting money away. It builds. You think it's going to be there when you retire. If that's the only thing you have access to, that's okay.

But you should know this: there is a reason why most people have mutual funds, especially open-ended mutual funds (exchange traded funds [ETFs] and closed-end funds are catching up). It's not because it's always in your best interest to own them or that mutual funds are always the best way to invest in the various investment markets. It's because big investment brokerage firms with the largest advisor sales forces are very expensive to operate. They have huge

BUY LOW, SELL HIGH, STUPID!

costs for employment, especially advisor training costs. How do they offset those costs? The national financial services firms that I worked for offset their training and recognition event costs by asking for and receiving substantial dollars primarily from mutual fund and insurance companies. They receive those dollars in exchange for being able to promote, excuse me, "educate" that big investment firm's advisors about their products. I call this "pay-to-play," although that would be wrong and not allowed, yet that is exactly how it works. In return for financial support, the large advisory firms give the mutual fund and insurance vendors special access to their financial advisors. When I was working in those big brokerage firms, it was very frowned upon for the financial advisors and sales managers like myself to sell outside of those preferred mutual fund vendor lists. The goal? To keep you investing your money in the company's mutual funds on the preferred mutual fund vendor list rather than consider other options.

Still, mutual funds have come a long way. I may not care for how they are promoted, and I strongly believe there are better, more efficient ways to build portfolios than open-ended mutual funds, such as with ETFs and closed-end funds. But I understand that open-ended mutual funds may be all you have access to right now until you retire, and that is okay. In the upcoming chapters, I'll share investment strategies and rules that you can use with mutual-fund-only portfolios too.

YOU DECIDE...

- You shouldn't expect less in retirement.
- Checking, savings, money markets, and CDs are not the best investments for a great return on your money.

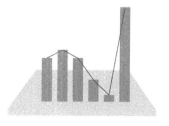

CHAPTER THREE

NEW PRODUCTS AND OFFERINGS

Many big investment firms are typically investment banks that underwrite and sell new proprietary offerings (such as bonds, stocks, and mutual funds) that they bring to market. And what distribution force do they use to bring those investments to market? Mostly their own. Their best sales-people are usually given the most shares to sell to the public or to their existing clients, which doesn't necessarily mean that the primary bond, stock, or mutual fund they're selling should be in your portfolio. But, overwhelmingly, that is exactly where most of their new investment offerings end up.

Do some of those proprietary investments do well? Yes, they do. But do you think it's fair for some people—those with less money—to not get the same access to all their investments or to be limited to what one firm thinks is best for you, which is more than likely just mutual funds? Usually, what a firm thinks is best for your portfolio is really best for them first—and you second. Now, large firms are not all so bad. But a lot of people haven't saved or accumulated the type of wealth to garner access to the best investment solutions that a larger firm and its salesforce has to offer.

> **USUALLY, WHAT A FIRM THINKS IS BEST FOR YOUR PORTFOLIO IS REALLY BEST FOR THEM FIRST—AND YOU SECOND.**

There's more to investing than just what typical financial advisors in the banking world and big brokerage houses would have you believe is your best path to retiring with more of what you need, not less than you need. If an investor with $1 million or more has high expectations for their returns, why shouldn't you? Why should somebody with less money not be afforded the same options?

There are ways for people with less income and fewer assets to make great returns. But all financial advisors are not created equally. And in fact, most are woefully underskilled and underexperienced and lack the ability—or are not allowed, even if they do have the ability—to utilize advanced or more complex solutions for their clients that are widely available to people with big money.

Now, before we move on to the nitty gritty, let me explain the difference between what's known as a *financial advisor* versus what's known as a *portfolio manager, in my opinion.*

YOU DECIDE...

- Even if you have less money, you shouldn't be satisfied earning less from your investments.

- Big banks and big investment firms don't necessarily have your best interests in mind.

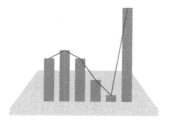

CHAPTER FOUR

FINANCIAL ADVISORS VERSUS PORTFOLIO MANAGERS

R ecently, through a referral, Nash came to see me because he felt that his financial advisor at a national firm wasn't being aggressive enough. In other words, Nash wasn't happy with the returns and performance he was getting on his investments. But for Nash to be more "aggressive" didn't mean he had to take on riskier investments to get better performance. Why not? Because all he really needed was better, more active management of what he had.

Why wasn't Nash getting better returns? Because he was going with a *financial advisor* versus a *portfolio manager*. Most investors don't understand the difference between the two, and it's an important one. Let me explain why.

First, let me start by explaining a crucial point: there are two types of management when it comes to your portfolio—passive management and active management. What's the difference?

Passive management is what financial advisors and most large national brokerages allow their advisors to employ. Passive management means that these financial advisors are not proactively changing your investments as necessary to keep you on track to achieve your goals. In order to be proactive, a financial advisor would have to be granted discretionary authority by you and their firm—they would have to be allowed to utilize their own discretion when making a portfolio decision for you, their clients. Since most advisors are not allowed to use discretion by their firm or their clients, they must operate on a reactive basis; they must first seek and then receive their client's authorization to make a change to their investment portfolio. They have to call up their client and say, "Hey, you should buy this mutual fund or this investment, or we should sell this mutual fund or this investment. What do you think? Do you want to do that?" Well, that's not great speed of business. That's not great service. That's not great value. Waiting for permission is a drastically inadequate advice-and-service model when it comes to managing money. If an advisor has to wait for their client to decide and authorize what to buy or sell for their account, what does the investor really need the advisor for? The answer: nothing. That would be like hiring a CPA and then telling them how to do accounting.

Big firms don't allow most of their financial advisors to make discretionary decisions about investing without having a number of years of experience and having successfully completed specialty training or credentialing. Financial advisors typically are only allowed to sell something from a preferred vendor list or stock buy list of the firm where they work. Sadly, most big-firm financial advisors are not qualified or allowed to utilize all the tools and abilities that are available to us portfolio managers.

Portfolio managers, on the other hand, manage money with a team on an active basis versus a passive basis. With active management, the portfolio manager uses discretionary authorization and trading ability; in other words, the portfolio manager decides what to buy and when to buy it. They custom build portfolios and are the ones who actually decide what specific investment to buy, when to buy it, when to sell it, and when to move on. They make daily decisions on portfolio assets, which may include stocks, bonds, mutual funds, ETFs, and alternative investments. That means they don't leave messages on your phone asking you for permission and then wait for you to call back, only to tell you: "I'm sorry. I didn't make that transaction that would have saved you from losing money or made you more money because I needed your permission. I was waiting for you to call me back to tell me it was okay." The qualifications, authorization, and use of discretion by portfolio managers are the biggest differences between them and a financial advisor.

EXPERIENCE, TRANSPARENCY, AND AN OBLIGATION TO WORK FOR YOU

When you hire a portfolio manager to manage your money directly, you are hiring that person to make the decisions for you. So experience, skill set, credentials, and success rate count. As a portfolio manager and principal, I've managed people's money or people who manage people's money through three market crashes and successfully helped them avoid losing money and often exceeded my client's income and growth goals net of fees.

Transparency is also key. At my firm, there are no hidden fees. We don't get investment product commission, so we are not incentivized to sell you specific investment products. And by charging fees, not working on commission, we have a fiduciary relationship with our clients. As a fee-only investment advisory firm and portfolio manager with discretionary authority, we are required legally to act in the best interest of our clients.

> **AS A FEE-ONLY INVESTMENT ADVISORY FIRM AND PORTFOLIO MANAGER WITH DISCRETIONARY AUTHORITY, WE ARE REQUIRED LEGALLY TO ACT IN THE BEST INTEREST OF OUR CLIENTS.**

Who typically works with a portfolio manager? People with a lot of money. But it doesn't have to be that way. I'll say it again: Why should you, with your hard-earned dollars, accept the status quo? Why should you settle for passive investing with a financial advisor when you can have a custom-created investment model that is proactively managed on a discretionary basis from a highly trained and experienced certified portfolio manager (CPM)? If you work with a portfolio manager, such as myself, we actually design a custom portfolio based on your specific goals on a proactive basis.

Now, knowing what you know, which would you prefer: a financial advisor who has to sell from a preferred vendor list and has to ask your permission before making a move? Or would you rather have a portfolio manager who is actively looking for ways to access more strategies that have potentially bigger returns usually enjoyed only by clients with more wealth?

YOU DECIDE...

Would you rather have:

- An active portfolio manager or a passive/reactive financial advisor?

- A custom portfolio or a common portfolio?

- A contrarian portfolio manager or a financial advisor who follows the status quo?

- A credentialed portfolio manager or an inexperienced financial advisor?

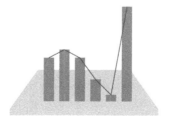

CHAPTER FIVE

BUY-AND-HOLD IS FOR SUCKERS

As I mentioned in the introduction, I spent a good portion of my career working for big investment brokerages as a manager responsible for billions of dollars in investments. During that time, I also trained other advisors and taught them all about the only strategy the firms promoted—buy-and-hold, no matter what. At that time, all those buy-and-hold investments were mostly mutual funds. ETFs and closed-end funds didn't exist. New mutual funds were coming to market every day. The funny thing is most of the growth mutual funds overlapped each other. They all had similar holdings: one growth fund from one company was the same as a growth fund from another company. The big investment advisory firms offering mainly mutual funds were birthed from that era, and the masses all received the same vanilla investment: a growth fund, bond fund, or growth-and-income fund. There was nothing special about them. If you held them for ten years, you might average a 10 percent return. But if the stock market dropped 40 percent, it took a whole lot of time to get back to where you were—time you might not have if you are close to retirement.

Too often, investments with the big financial groups are managed based on what I've shared with you previously, the idea that you should buy and hold the investment, no matter what happens and probably without true diversification. The last thing a large investment firm wants you to do is take your money out of the market. As a result, mutual funds are oversold and saturated, lack true diversification with a negative correlation to each other, and pose a substantial risk

HOLDING ON TO YOUR INVESTMENTS WITHOUT A CHANGE IN STRATEGY IS DETRIMENTAL TO YOUR NET WORTH.

to one's livelihood, in my opinion. Holding on to your investments without a change in strategy is detrimental to your net worth, especially when it comes to times like today with inflation about to explode, taxes on all fronts being potentially increased, and more and more tyrannical business regulations stifling our country. I'll say it again: buy-and-hold is for suckers. But that is what most financial advisors will tell you to do, especially ones at large financial institutions such as banks with brokerage arms that focus on their profitability first, then their shareholders', and their customers' dead last, despite what their phony-baloney mission statements say.

At my firm, we employ strategies to help you achieve more favorable overall results that focus on what's best for you first and us last. That's what we did for Joe, who I mentioned back in chapter 2. When he moved his portfolio to my firm, I sold off some of the bond funds in his portfolio to take profits because they had gone up in value, and further increases in value were not likely during the time of the writing of this book, plus the interest and dividends he was receiving were terrible. In a rising interest rate environment, you do not want to hold bonds or bond funds that hold bonds with long maturities. Also, you do not want to be holding onto growth stocks that aren't profitable and are highly leveraged, because rising interest rates and an inflationary economy will crush small company/growth stocks, and in many cases large company stocks too. I sold many of his investments focusing on positions that didn't pay any dividends to speak of. I turned around and bought large company value stocks with improving fundamentals plus beat-up stock ETFs in great sectors and very liquid, publicly traded medical property REITS (stay away from private right now) that were cheap, paying high dividends instead of the low-yielding investments Joe was told to hold on to. Had we not taken Joe on as a client and completely dismantled and rebuilt his portfolio prior to the coronavirus shutdowns, I think Joe would have lost 40 to 50 percent of his account's value compared to where he is sitting today up around 30 percent.

Don't be greedy or afraid to take profits. If you have made 20 percent, 30 percent, or more on a position in a short amount of time, please take some profit off the table and pay your taxes like the proud investor you are. Conversely, if you have properly diversified your portfolio not betting too much on any one position (more on that subject later), don't be afraid to buy a little more on down days into companies that you still believe in and want to own long-term.

DON'T BE GREEDY OR AFRAID TO TAKE PROFITS

I am not talking about becoming a day trader when I say buy-and-hold is for suckers. What I am advocating for is paying attention to your investments and what affects them. Again, if you are in bonds or bond funds, know that rising interest rates will hurt the value of your bonds and bond funds, so don't buy more in that environment or buy ultrashort maturities. Additionally, higher-interest rates, especially if caused by inflation (that we are starting to see now), are bad for stocks, especially small stocks. Those are simple examples of times when it is appropriate to take profits, increase cash, or at least rebalance your portfolio to investment classes and sectors that do well when everything is inflating. It pains me to suggest this, but if you are managing your own money, at least do an internet search for "investments that thrive during rising interest rates and high inflation."

Here's the thing: When your nest egg falls from $100,000 to $50,000, that's a 50 percent loss. To get back to $100,000, you need a 100 percent return.

Let me break it down: If you have $100,000, and it goes down 50 percent, you have $50,000. Many people think, *Well, since my portfolio dropped 50 percent, then it just needs to go back up 50 percent to be where it was.* Seems like a no-brainer. But that's not the case. If your $100,000 drops to $50,000, it has to double before it's back to where it was. In other words, it has to go back up 100 percent. At 10 percent per year, it will take ten years to make 100 percent to get you back where you were.

$$\$100,000 - 50\% = \$50,000$$
$$\$50,000 \times 10\% \times 10 \text{ years} = \$100,000$$

Not selling and locking in some profits on your highly appreciated investments, knowing inflation, taxes, and regulations are increasing, is for suckers.

Over a 40 percent drop just happened prior to me writing this book. By the end of April 2020, the Dow had dropped approximately

43 percent from its previous all-time high. It does happen and will happen again. But the point is that it doesn't have to happen to you. I don't want to see you have to potentially double your money to get back to where you were.

You would be kicking yourself if you watched your account go from $50,000 to $75,000 to $100,000, only to watch it go all the way back down to where you started in a blink because you've been taught to hold and never sell. Imagine how long it will take to get back to where you were if you're only averaging 5 to 7 percent return per year!

Most people never sell or change their investments in their 401(k) plan for long-term growth, and that is typically okay if you have more than five years to go at work. However, what I am saying is: do not buy a growth investment, watch it highly appreciate over the years, and never at least take your original investment off the table, especially if you're close to retirement or retired already. Because the market always goes up and down, and when it goes down, you can lose that original investment very quickly.

I am also not suggesting you become a day trader. Do I think you should spend your days dealing in short-term trades? No. But that's why you need to work with an active portfolio manager versus a passive financial advisor. An active portfolio manager will employ those simple strategies we have discussed so far to help you lock in your gains and potentially grow your account versus letting your account just go up in value, go down, and then take years to return. And you'll be in a position to invest even more because an active manager knows how to take your profit off the table and use it to invest more when appropriate.

In summary, portfolio managers like me do not passively buy and hold investments, waiting for something drastic to happen. Instead, they actively manage their clients' accounts. They know it's less risky to not overbet on any one position or let it ride when you have made a lot of money.

YOU DECIDE...

- Don't be afraid to take profits.
- You're not a day trader just because you're not following a strict buy-and-hold strategy.

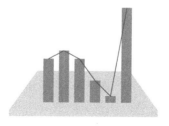

CHAPTER SIX

PLAYING WITH THE HOUSE'S MONEY

W e started talking about taking some profits off the table in the last chapter, but it's really important for your portfolio to thrive to take it a step further. Recently, on my radio show, I told our listeners to buy Amazon, which had dipped quite a bit after reporting incredible quarterly earnings. Only a few weeks later, Amazon went up several hundred dollars per share. Most people seeing those gains in their Amazon shares would hang onto that position for various reasons, such as not wanting to pay short-term capital gains tax or letting the green-eyed monster take over the management of their portfolio. The reality is that people are too emotional to manage their

> **THE REALITY IS THAT PEOPLE ARE TOO EMOTIONAL TO MANAGE THEIR OWN MONEY.**

own money. If I were a gambling man, I would bet that most people ride their stocks like Amazon back down. Ultimately, in a stock like Amazon, you'll probably be okay because I believe Amazon has more room to grow, especially its AWS or web services revenue and profits. We'll get into an actual portfolio model later.

If I was your portfolio manager, I would sell some of that Amazon position. Why? I want to be able to play with the house's money; I want to lock in some of those profits for your portfolio. I don't want to see you do what most people do and just ride all that profit back down to what it was, or worse, below the price you paid.

So do you get what I mean when I say to "play with the house's money"?

When you play games of chance—blackjack, craps, roulette—you might start with $1,000. After a few rounds of play, let's say that you doubled your money to $2,000. Half of that $2,000 is the money you started with, and half of that $2,000 is the house's money. When I say play with the house's money, what I mean is that, once your money has doubled or even had a healthy gain, take your original investment—in this case, your $1,000—off the table and put it in your pocket. Don't keep playing with it. Instead, keep playing with the money that you've gained—that's playing with the house's money.

It's the same concept when it comes to investing. The market is two-way: on the other side of your trade is an institution or person betting against you. Whether it's real estate, a stock, a bond, a car, there is a buyer and a seller in the transaction. If you're the buyer, there's a seller; if you're the seller, there's a buyer (not always). And in that transaction, each side is trying to win, to come out better than the other side. When it comes to investing, the only way you're a winner is by selling. At some point, if you never realize your gain, then you never win, technically speaking.

If you make an investment of $50,000 and it appreciates significantly, then take at least your original investment off the table or a substantial portion of it—lock in that win and play with the profits. At least then, if you ride it back down, then you haven't lost all your original investment.

Las Vegas casinos love people who don't pull their money off the table. They want you to keep playing with the original money you bring to the table because they know the odds are stacked in their favor. Why let the other side win? Instead, let's stack the odds in your favor.

Playing with the house's money strategy is simple, but you also need to learn another simple strategy known as dollar-cost averaging. For instance, let's say you buy one thousand shares of something at $10 per share; that's a $10,000 investment. Then that $10 per share goes up to $20 per share; now you have $20,000 in that investment. If you sell half of your position, or five hundred shares, at $20 per share, you've taken $10,000 off the table, but you still have $10,000 in that investment.

INITIAL INVESTMENT:
1,000 shares @ $10 per share = $10,000
$10 share increases to $20 share
1,000 shares @ $20 per share = $20,000
Sell 500 shares @ $20 per share = $10,000

VALUE:
$10,000 in remaining 500 shares,
$10,000 in your pocket

Now the market drops and that $20 per share goes down to $10 per share. If you take that $10,000 that you pulled off the table and invest it again, buying another 1,000 shares at $10 per share, you have 1,500 shares versus the 1,000 shares you started with. If that $10 per share goes back up to $15 per share, your investment becomes $22,500 instead of the original $10,000.

INITIAL INVESTMENT:
1,000 shares @ $10 per share = $10,000
$10 share increases to $20 share
Sell 500 shares @ $20 per share =
$10,000 in your pocket

VALUE:
$10,000 in remaining 500 shares at
$20, $10,000 in your pocket

SECOND INVESTMENT (OUT OF POCKET):
1,000 shares @ $10 per share = $10,000

VALUE:
1,500 shares @ $10 per share = $15,000
$10 share increases to $15 share

VALUE: 1,500 shares @ $15 per share = $22,500
Or $12,500 in profit

YOU DECIDE...

- Play with the house's money instead of buying and holding.

- Make sure that your advisor and the firm they work for has your best interest at heart.

- Do you want to invest like a pro, or should you hire a professional portfolio manager?

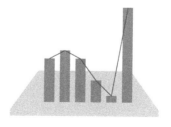

CHAPTER SEVEN

FINANCIAL PLANNING FOR DUMMIES

P eople often look to advisors with titles such as certified financial planners (CFP) or big Wall Street firms for financial planning and investment advice. The problem is that they end up paying a lot of money to get a comprehensive written document that often ends up filed away or tossed in the trash.

The truth is what they're paying for is pretty much common sense. I can summarize in a few minutes what almost all comprehensive plans will tell you, and I won't charge you a dime for it. Yet any plan is worthless without someone like me to help you execute the strategies necessary to ensure you create the income you need in retirement and that you don't outlive your money. It's preposterous to me that people pay a small fortune for someone to tell them that they need to pay off all their debts and save as much money as possible, to put so much weight in titles instead of hiring somebody who's actually going to execute the strategies in a plan to make money for you. Too many people don't understand that they're paying a onetime fee or annual fee for someone to update their written plan instead of directly hiring someone who will actually help them achieve the investment returns on their assets necessary to live off of in retirement.

WHEN YOU GET RIGHT DOWN TO IT, FINANCIAL PLANNING IS PRETTY SIMPLE.

When you get right down to it, financial planning is pretty simple—any dummy can do it:

1. You need income for retirement, and that takes good money management.

2. Don't go into debt; if you have debt, pay off all your debt, if you can, by retirement.

3. Mitigate life's financial risks. If you have insurance, great; if you don't have insurance, get some. You might need life insurance and/or disability insurance along with health, home, and auto.

4. If you need to pay for college for a child or grandchild, start saving as soon as possible.

5. If you have a sizeable estate, charitable aspirations, a legacy you want to leave, a special needs situation, create a will and trusts.

6. Hire a great accountant and an estate or elder law attorney, and most importantly, work with an active, highly experienced, fee-only investment management firm.

The reason I titled this chapter "Financial Planning for Dummies" is because anybody can and should have a plan. You just don't need to spend a lot of money for such a plan. Most investment advisory firms will create written goals and objectives as part of their investment management service. But a comprehensive financial plan guided or written by a "certified financial planner" is really, to me, in so many cases, just a lot of overblown marketing.

Many people shell out a ton of money for a written financial plan that ultimately results in a couple of pages of to-do items that they never follow or look at again. That's not helping you earn the money necessary to live a comfortable and confident life in retirement.

The true value is in the professional that you hire, someone who helps you understand what the items on those lists mean. Someone who not only lays out your goals and objectives but who also helps you reach them. Most investment advisory firms do help you create a plan for success in retirement or in the future. And most of the plans work toward several overarching themes: (1) retirement, (2) being debt-free, (3) risk mitigation, (4) college education, and (5) estate and legacy creation. Most plans help you establish goals and objectives for those elements. Some help you allocate resources for those goals and objectives. And most cost thousands of dollars and end up producing a multipage document that, again, just sits on a shelf somewhere in your home or office.

WHO IS ON YOUR SIDE?

To beat a dead horse, you don't need a CFP to tell you that you need to save money that will help pay for your retirement, pay off your debt, have more insurance to mitigate risk, plan for a college education, and have a will and a trust to help you leave a lasting legacy.

When I manage someone's money, my reputation and career are on the line. I'm going to help you get from point A to point B. More than just writing out a document, my team and I are going to help you execute what's in the document. With me on your side, your plan is not going to sit on a shelf and gather dust. It's going to be an evolving plan that changes along with you over time. As money managers, we do an analysis as part of our services to establish your personal goals and objectives. We look for pitfalls in your financial strategies and expectations. We look for ways to improve what you're doing and help you achieve your goals.

> **WHEN I MANAGE SOMEONE'S MONEY, MY REPUTATION AND CAREER ARE ON THE LINE.**

When it comes to financial planning, you know what you need to do. You know what's going to be in that financial planning book. You know you need to save or earn more money than 1 percent. You know you need to pay off your debt. You know you need enough income in retirement. Who's going to help you get that?

Financial planning is simple. Any dummy can do it. What you need is someone who will execute those plans for you—that's where I, and my team of money managers, come in.

YOU DECIDE...

- Financial planning is pretty simple—any dummy can do it.

- There are five basic pieces to financial planning.

- You need income for retirement that lasts your lifetime.

- Don't go into debt; if you have debt, pay off all your debt by retirement.

- Whenever possible, mitigate life's financial risks with insurance.

- If you need to help pay for your children's education, start saving as soon as possible.

- If you have a sizeable estate, charitable aspirations, a legacy you want to leave, a special needs situation, create a will and a trust.

- You need a financial professional who will help you execute what's in the plan.

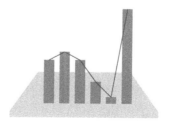

CHAPTER EIGHT

FEAR VERSUS GREED

R ecently, a client came in to see me because she was getting ready to retire. Her main concern was about how she could continue her lifestyle in retirement with the money she accumulated while working. She wanted to know what she could do with her account that would make her more money but would still keep her money relatively safe. "How do I ensure that I don't lose money?" she asked.

I had to break the news to her: "If you're in accounts that pay less than 1 percent, you're already losing money."

That's what most people don't understand. Every day that your money is in a low-return account, one that pays less than how much the cost of goods and services are increasing by annually, you're losing money. Why? Because of what I just described: inflation. The cost of inflation is continually raising the price of everything, and your low-return investments are not keeping pace with those increases. You're willing to lose buying power because of the fear of losing money, not realizing that your fear of losing money is coming true.

Think about it: Has there ever been a time in any given year where the cost of healthcare, energy, food, transportation, or just about anything hasn't gone up? These and every other aspect of life cost more every year. Certainly, we've seen healthcare costs drastically increase 50 percent or more, especially with the passing of the Affordable Care Act (ACA). The ACA alone touted that government-subsidized healthcare would allow you to keep your same doctor for less money. Right? Is that what happened? No. All the ACA did for many people was make healthcare costs go through the roof. If the costs of everything else increase at 3 to 5 percent a year or more, and all you're making is 1 percent or less on your investments, guess what? You're going to run out of money in retirement.

My point is this: You cannot let fear drive your investment strategy. Nothing out there will give you the returns you need without involving a bit of risk. If you're going to keep up with the prices of things as they increase, you can't put your money in something that, by definition, is 100 percent safe. If you do that, you're probably guaranteed to not have enough money during retirement. You're guaranteed to not keep pace with inflation. You're guaranteed to see your account dwindle down over your lifetime and possibly run out of money because (A) you didn't start with enough money and then (B) you didn't earn enough money on *that* money after you started needing it to supplement your lifestyle in retirement.

Most people around the country have not saved enough money for retirement. What is the worst thing you can do when you have not saved enough? Not earn enough on the money you have saved. So you must put your money in something that involves some risk. But there's a definite upside: it's called the risk-reward premium. That means investing in something that pays you for the risk you are taking. It means investing in something that is not guaranteed to be safe but that definitely has a strong potential to bring you a greater return, one that better than offsets the cost of inflation.

If you're in a portfolio that is properly diversified in various types of investments, and you've taken the appropriate amount of risk per position over a long period of time, you should never lose. You should average a minimum of 10 percent per year on your money. Why anyone would settle for earning less than 1 percent per year on their money, especially their retirement savings, makes absolutely no sense to me.

There's a misconception that once you're of a certain age and not working anymore, you have to be satisfied with a very low to zero return on your money. That's a fallacy. There is no reason on earth for you to settle for the idea that you have to live on far less. There's no reason to accept the idea that you'll run out of money in retirement and be dependent on the government to subsidize your needs. But that's what so many people believe because they don't want to invest in something that could potentially return what they need to pay for the rest of their lives, even after they are no longer working. It makes no sense, but it's based on a mindset that's been instilled in people for a long time. What it comes down to is the proper balance of fear versus greed. So as it was once said in the very famous movie *Wall Street*, "Greed is good." Get greedy!

FEAR VERSUS GREED

The masses have been taught to hate Wall Street. Mass media has told us time and again that Wall Street is where wealthy people are and that driving to create and have wealth is a bad thing.

What separates Main Street from Wall Street is the difference between fear and greed; Main Street (everyday people) operates on fear, and most of Wall Street operates on greed.

MAIN STREET (EVERYDAY PEOPLE) OPERATES ON FEAR, AND MOST OF WALL STREET OPERATES ON GREED.

When people think of Wall Street, they know it's an actual place in New York City, but they also immediately equate it with big money—the stock market, investment banks, corporations, investors, and big business and big profits. Simply, analysts on Wall Street focus on a company's earnings and guidance along with current and potential future economic conditions as the basis for making investments. What happens on Wall Street can and does impact the entire economy.

In short, Wall Street is the big money guys that don't settle for little to no returns on their clients' money, especially over a long period of time such as retirement. When it comes to Main Street versus Wall Street, we've been taught that Wall Street should always make more than Main Street. Wall Street should always be ahead of the curve when it comes to the markets going up or down, when to get in, when to get out. As the masses, we should just accept defeat and low returns. We should just accept not having wealth.

Well, I couldn't disagree with that more. You should be making a lot more money on your money—just like wealthy Wall Street clients and institutions.

TINA

There is an acronym that has driven me and my clients to great returns, one thing that overrides any thoughts about fear versus greed. That one thing? TINA—*there is no alternative* to investing in stocks.

If you're ever going to have a chance at beating or at least keeping up with inflation, you've got to think more like Wall Street than Main Street. You must face your fears and get greedy. You can't rely on money markets, certificates of deposit, and savings accounts alone to provide you a livelihood unless you have a vast fortune or an unlimited and indefinite income.

Most people have neither an indefinite income nor a vast fortune. If you're a normal Joe or Jane, then you really have no choice—you've got to remember the acronym TINA. You've got to make your investing decisions based more on greed than on fear; otherwise, how are you going to pay your bills in retirement? If you've only saved a couple hundred thousand, and you're counting on Social Security for the rest of your retirement income, then you can't invest based on the fear of losing money.

Let's say you've got $400,000 saved and put away, you need $5,000 a month to live on in retirement, and you're counting on Social Security of $2,000 per month. That means you're going to need $3,000 a month. If you take that $400,000 and approach investments with the emotion of fear, then even if you get a 3 percent return on risk-free investments, that's $12,000 per year or $1,000 per month, which is short $2,000 per month. However, if you take that $400,000, and we create a strategy that earns you 10 percent per year or more net of fees, that's $40,000 per year. That's $3,000 plus a month. Now add in the $2,000 from Social Security, and you've just replaced your $5,000 income.

Now, investing and getting those returns is definitely more technical and more detailed than just not being afraid to take some risk when investing (because, again, there is no alternative to stocks). But that's what you need someone like me for. For instance, as I'm writing this portion of the book, the markets have sold off a bit for profit. Investors are worried that the market will keep going down and they will lose all their money, so they're overreacting and moving everything to cash. But what should we do when the market goes down with investments we like and still believe have a prosperous future ahead? Buy more. *Buy low, sell high*. Instead of moving money over to cash, what these investors should be doing is buying more of whatever investments they have for their retirement from cash. You should always have cash as part of your portfolio, as we will discuss in more detail.

Again, you should never be satisfied with earning less than inflation or what you need to earn on your money to accomplish your goals and think that's a great strategy for retirement. If you're afraid of the markets because you or your previous advisor lost you money, well, I've got news for you: you're already losing money, as we have discussed.

Here's what it boils down to: I deliver to Main Street what Wall Street does for people with big wealth. I'm fighting to give Main Street what Wall Street gets. If you're Wall Street, you're big; if you're Main Street, I want you to think like Wall Street.

The keys to the kingdom are yet to come. When you work with me or with any portfolio manager worth a grain of salt, you should never be in a position of fear. You should always be comfortable with what your investments are doing for you and how they are helping you maintain your station in life and get through all the financial challenges that may result as you age.

YOU DECIDE...

- What is the worst thing you can do when you have not saved enough? Not earn enough on the money you have saved.

- Fear is why people accept low returns.

- You cannot accept low returns. If you're going to keep up with the prices of things as they increase, you can't put all your money in low-yield accounts.

- Don't accept lower levels of expertise and opportunity because you aren't an extremely wealthy Wall Street customer.

- Remember the abbreviation TINA: *there is no alternative to stocks.*

CHAPTER NINE

MAKING MONEY ON YOUR MONEY

I believe it was Warren Buffett who came up with the following two simple investing rules: Rule 1, "Never lose money." And Rule 2? "Never forget rule number one."

Now that's easy to say and tougher to do. So how can you "never lose money" and, better still, make great money on your money?

For starters, you need to understand what's known as your minimum return to objective (MRO). Your minimum return to objective is looking at the amount of return your investments need to generate to give you the lifestyle you want to maintain in retirement.

Let's say you need an income of $100,000 in retirement. Now, some of that will come from Social Security, maybe some will come from a pension. But your main retirement asset that you have to generate income on is your 401(k), which you plan to rollover to an IRA that has $800,000. Let's keep the math simple and say that you need $80,000 per year from your IRA to get to the $100,000 that you need in income before taxes. If your objective is to have income of $80,000 a year from your IRA, then you need a return of 10 percent, or $6,667 per month from your $800,000. We have just created an MRO goal of 10 percent.

A KEY WAY TO ENSURE YOU MEET YOUR RETIREMENT GOALS IS TO UNDERSTAND THE USE OF "LEVERAGE."

Obviously, to get that MRO, 100 percent of your money can't be in the bank in a money market or a certificate of deposit or a savings account. Because, as you know, and if you're lucky, you might get 1 percent on your money in a bank. At 1 percent on $800,000, that's $8,000 per year or $667 per month—that's more than a little shy of the $6,667 per month that you need.

So how can you reach your MRO? A key way to ensure you meet your retirement goals is to understand the use of "leverage."

What exactly is leverage? For starters, know that leverage is the key to being able to access other strategies that typically the very wealthy have access to because they have high income and tons of capital. Some of those strategies using leverage fall into a category of investments known as alternatives.

Let me digress just a bit before we go into the use of leverage. One of the most important things to being a successful money manager for yourself or other people's money is always being in a position to buy something on sale that has the potential to appreciate, add income, or do both to your portfolio. That goes back to Buffet's quote about never losing money; the way I interpret what he said is to always be in a position with cash to buy when the time is right. My client's portfolios always have cash, money markets, and/or ultrashort income funds as part of a client's allocation to ensure two things: (1) you always are in a position to be a buyer, and (2) you are never 100 percent invested in the markets. I'll talk more in depth about the allocation of your portfolio in the next chapter.

ALTERNATIVE STRATEGIES

First, I am not talking about leveraged funds or ETFs. As part of the leveraging strategies at my firm, we believe in using strategies that, in my opinion, the majority of typical advisors don't know how to do or aren't allowed to do with the clients that they have in their division. What alternative strategies am I referring to? The use of options contracts. In order to have options in your portfolio, you must maintain a margin or loan account. That does not mean you have to borrow (leverage) your account to have options in your portfolio, and at my firm we do not leverage our clients' positions or accounts.

Options contracts are one of the most misunderstood types of investments. Most of the investing public, including your typical financial advisors, are woefully misinformed when it comes to some of the simple portfolio strategies with options, such as enhancing the income of a low-dividend and interest-paying portfolio. Sadly, just the word "options" has people heading for the hills when the use of what are known as "covered calls" doesn't necessarily add any more risk to a portfolio than owning the stocks to begin with. In fact, options can also be used to protect profits or hedge a position, actually reducing certain types of risk.

SIMPLIFYING OPTIONS*

So how exactly do options work, you ask? Let me share just a few insights about these types of investments, starting with some terms.

There are two types of options: calls and puts. If you own call options, you are bullish on the stock (you want the stock to go up in price), and if you own put options, you are bearish on a stock (you want the stock to go down in price). Both types come with an expiration date. With a call option, you have the right to purchase a stock at a strike (or set) price on or before its expiration date. With a put option, you can potentially sell a stock at the strike price on or before its expiration date (American style). For example, if I own an Apple call option with a strike price of $100 and an expiration date of January 2022, I can exercise my option anytime on or before January 2022 to buy a hundred shares of Apple stock at a cost of $10,000 ($100 strike price x one hundred shares per contract = $10,000). If Apple stock is above $100 per share, that means your Apple call option is "in the money" and you can sell your Apple call potentially for a nice profit.

Conversely, if Apple stock is trading below $100 and I own (long) an Apple $100 put, my put option is "in the money," and I can sell my Apple put option potentially for a nice profit. Simply buying options on a stock per contract is typically far less per contract than buying a hundred shares of the underlying stock. Why would someone want to buy an option on a stock instead of actually buying the stock? I'll tell you why: *leverage*.

Just like stocks, options involve risk. Let's take a look at buying a simple call option on a stock like Amazon. If I believe Amazon is going to go up in value (and I do), then I can buy the stock or buy

---

* Ninety percent of clients will not utilize options, as they are used for very specific situations only.

call options on Amazon stock. A hundred shares of AMZN currently takes $357,000 ($3,570 per share x one hundred shares), which most investors cannot afford. Conversely, I can buy one January 2022 AMZN $3,500 call for a premium of $320 per contract per share or $32,000, or less than one-tenth the cost of buying the stock. Now, if AMZN stock goes up $100 per share and, for education purposes, let's say the premium on my AMZN call option goes up by $100, then my AMZN stock is now worth $367,000 and my call contract is worth $42,000. Which return on investment do you like better? I like the return on the call option better, how about you?

There are many incredible investment strategies when it comes to options, such as covered calls and credit spreads to name a couple. Covered calls and credit spreads are a bit more complex than just buying a call or put. However, covered calls and credit spreads can be powerful income tools that we can use in clients' custom portfolios in order to achieve potentially higher returns necessary to accomplish their goals. Let's take a look at a common covered call strategy.

Many of our clients are retired from publicly traded companies where they have accumulated, often, thousands of shares in their former company's stock, usually at a very low cost base. So let's assume you have three thousand shares of UPS stock that you earned over a twenty-year period working for UPS that you don't want to sell because of the tax burden it would trigger. UPS pays a dividend; however, in this example the dividend is not enough to meet my client's monthly income needs. So what can we do to help increase the income in our client's UPS portfolio? We can sell out of the money call options.

As I write this, UPS is trading at $211 per share with a fifty-two-week high of $219 and low of $117 (rounded to the nearest hundred). UPS is closer to its high than its low, and our client is very comfortable selling UPS call options where the risk is that she may have her UPS shares called away at a substantial profit, which would trigger a large capital gains tax. Now, there are strategies that we use to prevent her stock from being called away, but to keep things simple we aren't going to delve into that because I could write an entire book on the use of options in a portfolio, and I might. I love stocks with weekly option contracts like UPS. When we moved her UPS shares from Computershare to a brokerage account that we manage for her, the account started with just the shares (no cash). In less than one year, we created $89,000 in cash dividends and options premiums, which has increased the value of her portfolio by 24 percent after she took out $11,000 and net of our fee, plus the year isn't over yet. Not too shabby.

If you have a large portion of your net worth in a single stock, I highly suggest you work with a portfolio manager skilled in the utilization of options to help you protect your position and create income for you that you may not be getting now, especially if you refuse to sell your former or current company shares.

For our larger client portfolios, we like credit spreads. By the way, any strategy and positions you or we put into your portfolio should be a small percentage of your overall total portfolio, especially when using options. With that said, credit spreads are by far and away my most favorite income strategy. A credit spread is simply buying an option (long) and selling an option (short) on the same stock where the premium received for the short option is more than the premium you paid for the long option. That sounds complicated, but I can assure you it is not. Based on the title of this book, we are not going much deeper than that because I want you to finish the book. We utilize simple credit or short (not naked) options strategies because we like the odds of keeping some or all of the options premium we receive better than the odds of the premium we paid increasing enough to be profitable before your options expire (time decay). Think of this strategy like playing cards for money. It is better to be the dealer than it is to be the gambler. In the case of options, that means there's a greater chance of keeping the income or premium you receive for selling someone the right to call away your stock or sell you stock. With selling options, we have found that we can create a probability of close to 80 percent success for keeping some or all of the income or premium received. It's not guaranteed but neither is buying stocks to begin with.

Sounds complicated? It's really not. Sounds risky? It is risky, but there is less of your capital at risk for the strategies I described when buying or selling options than say buying a hundred shares of Amazon for over $300,000. Plus, utilizing option contracts creates a potential return on your investment that you just can't typically get. The options strategies we utilize have been used by portfolio managers like me for wealthy and aspiring to be wealthy clients for decades. The fact that most advisors and most average people have no knowledge or true understanding of options solutions never ceases to amaze me.

YOU DECIDE...

- As Warren Buffet said: Rule 1—never lose money; Rule 2—never forget Rule 1.

- MRO is about the amount of return your investments need to generate to give you the lifestyle you want to live in retirement.

- Leverage as we use it can be a powerful investment tool.

- The use of options* is an alternative investment strategy that can help enhance a portfolio's overall results.

- The average person's investment portfolio is not properly diversified with too much capital at risk in any one investment.

- A disciplined approach to investing can help you mitigate potential losses and increase potential return on investment.

---

* Only a very few of our clients have options in their portfolio and their use is limited to very specific individual client situations where their use may be appropriate.

60

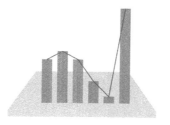

CHAPTER TEN

INCREASE INCOME WHILE DECREASING RISK

O ne of the top mistakes that people make when it comes to their retirement portfolios is this: they don't get paid for their time. They're so fearful of the markets that they put the majority of their money in investments that don't pay them an appropriate amount of return for the length of time they own the investments—and certainly not an appropriate amount of money yielded from their investments for their income needs in retirement. They invest in things that don't pay them while they're waiting for that investment to go up in value, meaning it doesn't yield anything but the potential to appreciate. That's a big mistake. Why would you do that? If you're going to invest your money, you need to get a return on that investment the entire time you own it.

Real estate is a good way to demonstrate what I mean. If you own a rental home and you never rent it, you're not getting paid for your time. Your only hope on making money on that particular investment is for it to go up in value. Well, that's a big mistake in my opinion. If you have a rental property, it needs to be rented for it to be a great overall return on investment.

But that same understanding often does not translate to other investments, particularly stocks or bank investments. People often just bet that they've picked the next great, undervalued company that will go up in value. They don't even look at whether that stock they bought pays dividends. Yet you'd have to be a clairvoyant to know with certainty whether a stock is going to go up and net you the return you need when selling the investment for a gain.

One of the things I regularly witness from go-it-alone investors, besides not getting paid for their time, is that they are taking too much risk with their money—and receiving the right premium or reward for the investment risks they are taking. They may be in stock funds, individual stocks, bond funds, or individual bonds. Regardless of the type of asset, they're not getting paid for the high risks that they're taking.

WE DON'T TAKE TOO MUCH RISK—NOR DO WE RECOMMEND TAKING NO RISK.

That's where my firm comes in. We align people's investments with the actual returns that are needed for them to meet their MRO so that they can maintain their station in life. We don't take too much risk—nor do we recommend taking no risk. We base the risk in your portfolio on your MRO. Again, MRO, or minimum return on objective, is a planning technique that you need to know: What is your benchmark? How well do your investments or portfolio need to do based on that number or personal benchmark?

Most people are one of two things: they're either underinvested or overinvested. When you're underinvested, you don't have enough risk premium in your portfolio—the rates of return that you're earning aren't consistent with the minimum rate of return that you need to accomplish your goals. Too much risk, or being overinvested, means that you've got too much of your money in a particular investment, like a company's stock that has recently gone public, and you bet the farm on it. It is rare that an investor is taking the appropriate amount of risk for the return that they need to generate the income they need, whether that be in retirement or whether that be the number that they need to get to their growth goal so that they can retire.

For example, let's say you need an annual income of $80,000 per year in retirement, and you have $1,000,000 in your retirement account. If you're underinvested and you're going to get anywhere near your $80,000 per year, you need an 8 percent minimum return to achieve that $80,000 per year in order to maintain your same station. Where are you going to average an 8 percent return? Remember TINA, *there is no alternative to stocks*. You're going to have to take calculated risks to consistently earn 8 percent. I have good news! If you have absorbed anything in this book so far then you know how important it is to get paid for your time. With high dividend-paying stocks, which are often highly profitable companies that are trading at a discounted valuation (good time to buy) pay 5 percent to as high as 14 percent in annual dividends. If you need 8 percent, it is not difficult, although not guaranteed, to build a portfolio averaging 6 percent in yield or more. Furthermore, if you focus on valuation too, you could realistically see upside of 5 percent or more kicking your average annual return above 10 percent, which is what the stock market has averaged through correction and crashes in any given decade.

Remember, in order to never lose money as your number one rule—as Warren Buffet may have said—your portfolio needs to be properly allocated and diversified among the various types of investments. You don't want to be underinvested, and you don't want to be overinvested: either way, you could potentially run out of money. If you're overinvested, you can lose too much money, and if you are underinvested then you aren't earning enough, and you are living on principal that will eventually run out. Furthermore, it's always better to be in a position to be a buyer prior to dips or corrections in the market rather than having to sell a position at a loss to buy something that might be a better value. Let's take a look at a sample growth and income model portfolio.

GROWTH AND INCOME CORE MODEL

At our firm, we follow some basic rules for selecting, building, and rebalancing the positions in a person's portfolio.

Again, we start by establishing your minimum return to objective. Let's again say in retirement you need an 8 percent return on $1 million that you have accumulated. Once again, many investors are either overinvested (too much risk in their portfolio) or underinvested (not enough risk premium in their portfolio). Most of our prospective clients generally are overinvested in stocks without proper diversification. If you're one of those people, then I have news for you: you don't have to put 100 percent of your money at risk in any one market such as stocks to get that net 8 percent return. What you need is a combination of many things to achieve your 8 percent objective. In fact, we typically get people to their minimum return to objective with up to 50 percent of their money in less-aggressive, completely liquid investments. How do we do that? We create and actively rebalance portfolios that go well beyond just owning passive stock and bond mutual funds that often pay little to no dividends.

STOCKS

Right now, we believe approximately 40 percent of a portfolio should be in individual stocks and stock ETFs, in our opinion, again focusing on stocks that are undervalued and pay dividends. As I was putting together this book, most of the stocks that our clients owned were bringing in 5 percent or more in dividends. It is not uncommon for companies that are experiencing financial difficulty to cut their dividends, which is one of the main indicators and reason to quickly remove that position from your portfolio. For example, in 2019 to sometime in 2020, many of our core client portfolios held Wells Fargo (WFC) that was paying approximately a 7 percent dividend, and when shit hit the fan in 2020, Wells discontinued paying its dividend and its stock started to fall in price. We sold out of WFC, and we bought JP Morgan (JPM) to stay in banking, which we believed would rebound, and it did, plus AT&T (T). We still have both in most portfolios today. JPM was paying around a 5 percent annual dividend at the time of purchase and has appreciated nicely in price since then. T has been consistently paying its quarterly dividend at an annual rate actually above 7 percent on an annual basis.

BONDS

As I write this, our portfolios have only 10 percent in investment-grade short and ultrashort-term bond ETFs. The reason we're only

10 percent in short-term bond investments is because with interest rates so low, prices of bonds have been way too high (at a premium) to increase our allocation percentages of bonds in our core growth and income client portfolios. The other reason for allocating some of your money to short-term and ultrashort-term bond ETFs is because the current yields annually of around 1 percent are better than cash yields of 0.05 percent.

REAL ESTATE INVESTMENT TRUSTS

We think up to 20 percent of your portfolio should be allocated to publicly traded, very liquid REITs, focusing on REITs that buy healthcare-type properties. We do not currently invest in REITs that primarily own high-rise class-A office space or traditional shopping malls. Instead, look to REITs that invest in medical facilities of any variety, warehouses, prison (yes, prison), and manufacturing and distribution properties. You can expect between a 6 percent and a 10 percent dividend from your REITs. There are some mortgage-backed securities (MBSs) REITs that have been paying above 10 percent, and it would be okay to have a sprinkling of those too. Keep in mind that should the Fed stop its buying of MBSs and interest rates on home loans shoot up, we could see defaults on loans again, which would cause MBS REITs to drop sharply in price. Another thing to keep in mind, many REITs follow or are highly correlated with the overall stock market, so be careful when buying REITs that you do not take on too much risk when combined with the money you allocated to stocks in your portfolio.

ALTERNATIVE STRATEGIES

Consider allocating up to 10 percent of your money to alternative strategies such as with the use of options*. I explained a couple of options strategies that we like to employ when appropriate in our client portfolios in the previous chapter. I intend to delve a bit further into the use of options in future chapters, but I also might write an entire book on making money with options*.

CASH

We increase and decrease the amount of cash in our portfolios based upon our belief in the various markets being overvalued or undervalued. Right now we believe the stock market to be overvalued based on several economic headwinds such as inflation, which has warranted us to allocating more money to cash or cash-like investments. Most people have too much capital at risk in my opinion with the stock market breaking all-time highs, interest rates at record lows, and inflation starting to raise its ugly head, which will eventually affect publicly traded companies' profitability, which in turn will put pressure on the stock market. Remember, know what your MRO is so that you don't take on more risk than necessary to get to your MRO. Some people have accumulated enough assets or passive income from pensions and other sources such as Social Security where they don't need to put any of their discretionary savings at risk. However, the average investor and/or retired person does not enjoy that level of prosperity after they retire.

Right now, having 30 percent of your money in cash is extremely important because you should always be in a position to buy an invest-

---

* Only a very few of our clients have options in their portfolio and their use is limited to very specific individual client situations where their use may be appropriate.

ment if the timing is appropriate versus having to sell another investment to do so because you could potentially be selling that investment at a loss. There's no reason to buy an investment with the money that you're taking out of another investment at a loss, assuming you did not invest too much money in any one position to begin with, which we will talk about more.

At my firm, our disciplined approach to managing and allocating people's money also includes these two very basic rules:

- No more than 50 percent in any one classification of investment: stocks, bonds, real estate, cash, etc.

- No more than 5 percent to start in any one position in each one of those classifications

Let's again say you have amassed $1 million: 40 percent of that will be in stocks (less than 50 percent in that classification), or $400,000 worth of stocks. Of that $400,000, holding to the "no more than 5 percent in any one position to start" rule means that no more than $50,000 will be in any one asset. Of that $1 million to start (5 percent), we feel it is important to have at least $200,000 (20 percent) in cash, and if you are anticipating troubled waters ahead for the stock market (no one has a crystal ball), you might want to decrease your stocks to 30 percent and increase your cash to 30 percent.

Here is a sample asset allocation.

SAMPLE CUSTOM ALLOCATION
ACTIVELY REBALANCED

ASSET CLASS	WEIGHTING	DIVIDEND OR INTEREST ANNUAL YIELD
Stocks	40%	5% to 7%
Bonds	10%	1% to 3%
REIT	20%	6% to 8%
Alternatives	10%	15% to 25%
Cash	20%	.05% to 1%
Approximate weighted variable annual yield: **7%** (not including growth)		

Finally, when it comes to making money on your money, remember: buy low, sell high. That's a key driver behind why we never start with more than 5 percent in any one position. Why? Well, we're not clairvoyant. For instance, with stocks, we don't know what the market's going to do—except that it's going to go up and it's going to go down. If it goes down and we like the company that we started investing in, we'll add to it versus sell it. And that, in turn, actually will give us a lower overall price through the use of the concept dollar-cost averaging. Whereas when too many people buy a stock, then it goes down, they panic and they sell. Did they buy low, sell high? No. What did they do? They bought high and sold low. And that is the most fundamental, emotional problem that people have when investing for themselves.

ACTIVE MANAGEMENT TO BALANCE CORRELATION

If you find you can't seem to take the emotion out of your investing behaviors, then what you need is a portfolio manager that actively adjusts and rebalances your positions within the model. Someone who proactively versus reactively manages your portfolio and follows the simple rules and strategies discussed so far.

For instance, on a $500,000 portfolio, using our model, 40 percent—or $200,000—would be in stocks. If we initially focus on being no more than 5 percent in any one position, that means taking on positions at an amount up to $25,000. Again, looking at that $200,000, which is 40 percent of the overall value of the portfolio, you're going to need at least eight positions to make up that $200,000. You certainly can start with less than $25,000 per position. We often buy and recommend that you buy 2 to 3 percent of your portfolio initially into a position and then see what happens. Right now, the market, especially growth stocks, is very volatile, so we are not starting with 5 percent. Be patient, buy little pieces, and see what happens.

Proper diversification can help reduce the downside risk in your portfolio, because if one position is having a really bad day or a really bad year, it doesn't mean that all the positions are having a really bad day or year.

In addition to not overinvesting in any one position, look at the sectors your investments fall under—such as consumer goods, pharmaceuticals, entertainment, wireless or internet companies, etc.—and don't invest all your money in stocks in the same sector. Also, being mindful of your stocks' correlation coefficient and beta to the S&P 500 can help increase your portfolio's chances for success. A positive correlation coefficient of 1.0 between two stocks means those two stocks will go up or down in the exact proportion. A negative correlation coefficient among your stocks of −1.0 simply means that prices on two different stocks will move in the exact opposite direction of each other. A beta of 1.0 means your stock will go up and down, dollar for dollar, with the S&P 500. If the stock's beta is higher than 1.0, it will go up or down more than what the S&P 500 goes up or down. If the beta of a stock is less than 1.0, it will go up or down less per dollar than the S&P 500. Don't fret—this information is widely available usually within your trading platform of choice or typically for free on sites like Yahoo Finance and many others.

With active management, we pay attention to the sectors we are investing in or trying to stay away from. We also look at a stock's correlation coefficient to stocks currently in our portfolio as well as a stock's beta. As I was writing this, consumer staples, industrials—materials, banking, and energy sectors of that nature—were up in the stock market. However, technology stocks went down. If we had all technology stocks, all our client's portfolios would be down. I'm happy to say that is not the case.

Here is a sample of the sectors and strategies we liked at the time I wrote this.

SAMPLE CUSTOM PORTFOLIO SECTORS

STOCKS	BONDS	REITS	ALTS
E-commerce	Ultrashort ETFs	Distribution	Covered calls
Materials	High yield 1 to 5 years	Hospitals	Naked puts
Industrials	Inv grade 1 to 5 years	Rehab	Credit spreads
Bio tech		Warehouse	
Internet security		Mortgage-backed sec.	
Cloud storage			
Pay services			
Semiconduc-tor			
3-D printing			

INCREASE INCOME WHILE DECREASING RISK

Based on our balanced allocation sample and the sample portfolio sectors, here's a sample portfolio:

POSITION SYMBOL	PRICE	52 HIGH/ LOW	VOLUME	YIELD
Stock				
DOW	$68	$21 to $56	27M	5.59%
EPD	$23.71	$15 to 24$	4M	7.56%
XOM	$58	$31 to $64	19M	5.90%
HTGC	$17	$5 to $17	289K	10.90%
IDE	$12	$6 to $12	50K	9.68%
IBM	$144	$106 to $149	4M	4.58%
JPM	$162	$88 to $165	9M	2.24%
Bond				
USIG	$59	$58 to $62	483K	2.76%
ICSH	$50.50	$50.45 to $50.60	283K	.83%
HYS	$98.92	$88 to $99	130K	4.40%
MINT	$101.98	$100.91 to $102.16	482K	.76%

POSITION SYMBOL	PRICE	52 HIGH/ LOW	VOLUME	YIELD
REIT				
NRZ	$10.25	$6 to $11	4M	7.71%
CSWC	$24.92	$12 to $25	60K	6.77%
MPW	$21	$16 to $22	4M	5.33%
REM	$36.57	$22 to $37	387K	6.02%
ALT* Strategy				
AAPL	$151	$112 to $157	51M	.59%
Buy AAPL Sept 2022 145 Call	$18.85			
Sell AAPL Nov 2021 160 Call	$0.53			25%

Credit spread return assumes keeping 75% of the premium received each month the short call is rolled for 12 consecutive months. The hypothetical illustration also assumes the premium received each month will be approximately the same. It also does not reflect whether the long call was sold for an eventual profit or loss. Figures in the table are rounded to the nearest dollar. Ninety percent of clients will not have options of any kind in their portfolio.

---

* Only a very few of our clients have options in their portfolio and their use is limited to very specific individual client situations where their use may be appropriate.

YOU DECIDE...

- Too many people make the mistake of not getting paid for their time when it comes to investing.

- Portfolios are often underinvested (not taking enough risk) or overinvested (taking too much risk).

- The core growth and income model is:

  - Stocks—40 percent

  - Bonds—10 percent

  - REITs—20 percent

  - Alternative strategies—10 percent

  - Cash—20 percent

- No more than 50 percent in any one classification of investment: stocks, bonds, real estate, cash, etc.

- A positive correlation coefficient means that all the investments go up and down together; a negative correlation coefficient means the prices move in the opposite direction.

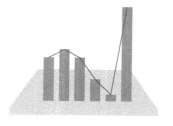

CHAPTER ELEVEN

FAIR AND TRANSPARENT

R ecently, we were referred a new client who had considerable financial means. She had an emergency situation though where she needed a very large lump sum of money to pay for some large unexpected expenses. We learned that she had been sold several variable annuity products by her bank, and she wanted to see about pulling money out of them for some hefty bills. In looking over her investments, we found out that taking the money out of her annuities would cost her gigantic back-end commission surrender charges—to the tune of $50,000, which she was not aware of! Fortunately, she was able to make other payment arrangements that were less costly until the surrender charges went away.

Her situation was something we see all the time. Banks sell thousands of annuity contracts every year, and their advisors typically do a very poor job of explaining what the investor is actually buying.

On top of that, many of the people we see that are loaded up with annuities are elderly people—seventy years old or older—because they are primarily the ones who have a lot of money sitting in a bank and still walk into a branch and bank the old-fashioned way.

We also helped another fairly new-to-us elderly client liquidate an A share mutual fund to the tune of $500,000, which the client was not aware she paid an upfront commission of 5.75 percent. Worse, she had not heard from her advisor in years, and she was not aware she was in 100 percent stock growth funds. The good news is we were able to help her get out of the funds and lock in a nice profit while the market was at record highs.

Why do so many people have open-ended mutual funds and annuities? Because of the high commission structure of these products that is usually not explained well by the person who sold them the investment products.

HOW YOUR ADVISOR IS PAID—IT MATTERS

I named this chapter "Fair and Transparent" because that's what it should come down to when looking at how your financial advisor or money manager gets paid. Fair and transparent is about disclosure of fees and commissions. How does the advisor and/or the firm make money off of you as the client?

FAIR AND TRANSPARENT IS ABOUT DISCLOSURE OF FEES AND COMMISSIONS.

Some financial products, such as annuities, are sold with a commission tied to them, which is paid by the product creator to the advisor who sells the product. But here's the deal: that product creator expects to recoup that commission. And guess who ultimately pays for it? The buyer of the product (that's you, the client/investor). When certain products are sold, that commission is typically structured in one of two different ways. Sometimes, it's paid by the client upfront. Sometimes, it is paid out to the advisor or the salesperson over time and tied to a surrender charge.

My intent is not to come down too hard on commission-based salespeople. As long as the advisor or firm explains how the commission structure works and the client understands and agrees to it, then it's okay to assess that kind of a fee. As long as the transaction is transparent. But often that's not the case. In fact, I personally think that commission structure incentivizes sales professionals to do the wrong thing, to not have the client's or the potential client's best interests at heart because they've got to sell something to generate a commission in order to get paid.

It's especially a problem when it comes to some insurance products—specifically annuities.

The problem with annuities is that they have those surrender periods I mentioned. The surrender period is the length of time—usually a pretty long length of time—that the investor must stay in annuity before being able to withdraw funds without a penalty. Surrender periods are commonly seven years or more, but they can go as long as twenty years—that's twenty years that you have to be invested in the same product. Withdrawing money before the end of the surrender period can result in the investor paying surrender charges. They are called surrender charges, but what they really are is reimbursement to the vendor, in this case the insurance company; the investor basically has to pay the insurance company the commission that the agent received for selling the product.

There are situations where annuities can be a decent investment. They can make sense if a person doesn't have a trust and doesn't want their money to go through probate; when interest rates are high (something we haven't seen in quite a while); or for high-tax-bracket individuals who are ineligible to contribute to typical retirement accounts. But again, they come with those potentially very long surrender penalty periods.

And as I mentioned earlier, the real problem I have with these types of products is that the commission is not typically explained well. That is not being transparent—and it's not being fair to the investor. Investors typically don't automatically understand the commission structure or how the commission is paid, and the contract, known as a prospectus, is usually long and filled with a lot of legalese—so much legalese that most people don't read them. They buy the product, throw the paperwork in a drawer, and never look back—until something happens, and they need funds.

MUTUAL FUNDS AND ANNUAL EXPENSE

There are mutual funds that work the same way as what I've explained with annuities, except that mutual funds are essentially shares of something. Here again, the client pays a commission upfront that goes to the advisor. For instance, if you have $100,000 in an A share mutual fund, the commission comes immediately out of your $100,000 upfront. So if it's a 5 percent commission, or $5,000, then that mutual fund actually starts out as $95,000.

B share mutual funds are commission-based mutual funds that act much like an annuity. The advisor gets paid by the mutual fund company and then the investor has a five- to six-year back-end commission surrender period. During that time period, the mutual fund company will recoup the commission paid to the mutual fund advisor in the form of a higher B share price than A price per share. With these, the commission surrender period is prorated on an annual basis if the client decides to get out of the mutual fund within the surrender period.

Another area where mutual funds are not transparent is an annual expense charge from the client's returns. That amount can be very little, such as ten basis points or one-tenth of 1 percent, or it can be very expensive, as much as 2 percent per year, depending on the type and brand of the fund.

Here again, that annual expense is something that is not explained very well. It's in the prospectus, all that legalese in the big, long contract that comes with the product, but very few people ever read all those details, and few ever ask the advisor: "How do you get paid?" "How much does this product or service cost me annually?"

To me, that's not being transparent. And it's not fair. It's not fair because of the incentive that it puts in the advisor's corner. It encourages advisors to try to sell clients something in order to get paid. If the investor is okay with the commission and expense structures, then it's not a problem. I mean, sellers deserve to be paid—it is fair to the sales professional, insurance agent, or money manager to be paid for the value they provide. But it's not fair to the client if that cost structure is not explained well.

There are big differences between firms—and also between the types of professionals at those firms—when it comes to transparency. At my firm, we don't sell commission-based products. We are fee-based that is very transparent and very fair.. We discuss everything with the client and disclose all fees. In my opinion, that is the only way to work with a firm or money manager to help you achieve your investment goals. They should be acting in a fiduciary capacity. They should be fair and transparent and explain very clearly how and what they get paid for managing your money. They should be working in *your* best interest—not in the best interest of themselves or of an annuity or commission-based mutual fund company.

YOU DECIDE...

- Many products are originally sold with a commission tied to them, whether that commission is paid by the client upfront or paid out to the advisor or the salesperson by the vendor upfront or over time and tied to a surrender charge.

- Withdrawing money before the end of the surrender period can result in the investor paying surrender charges. What that means is that the investor basically has to pay for any commission that was paid by the vendor to the agent selling the product.

- Commission-based investment products can and sometimes incentivize sales professionals to do the wrong thing, to not have the client or the potential client's best interests at heart because they've got to sell something to generate a commission in order to get paid.

- Commissionable products are not typically explained well. That is not being transparent or fair. Investors typically don't automatically understand the commission structure or how the commission is paid, and the contract, known as a prospectus, is usually long and filled with a lot of legalese that is never read by the investor.

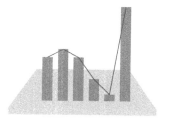

CHAPTER TWELVE

HOW TO GET STARTED

O ne of our newest clients is a couple who owns a franchise business. For twenty years, they have been investing everything they earned into their business. In the twentieth year, a major project at the company yielded the couple a windfall— a potential nest egg that they never had before. Up to that point, they hadn't really accumulated much in the traditional sense, not even as much as someone working for an employer and saving in an IRA or other traditional investment would have made during that same time.

Since their only investment at the time was their business, they had never really worked with any kind of financial institution or advisor other than traditional banks. The business had provided them with income over the years, but now in their sixties they realized that they were going to need to make money on the money they had accumulated. They were beginning to question whether to keep the business or sell it, considering the manual labor and stress involved in running it.

They came to see us at my firm to get some answers for how to make money off the lump sum that they now had—they had no idea how to get that money to yield an income that would be meaningful enough to let them retire. After a consult, they hired us, and I'm happy to say that, using the model that I've shared with you in this book, their return is expected to yield them an income on an annual basis greater than the income they took from the business each year.

WHEN IT COMES TO GETTING STARTED, YOU MUST FIRST DETERMINE WHAT SUCCESS LOOKS LIKE FOR YOU.

If they had just relied on the lump sum alone, depositing it in a bank as they had done with their income over all those years, then they would not have come close to having an income in retirement that met their needs. That lump sum alone would not have given them their MRO.

This couple's story demonstrates that it's never too late to learn and change the way you have always done things. You should always make money on your money. If investing in the various markets is something you've never done before, then it's a good idea to rely on a firm or individual who really knows what they're doing. Someone who will take the time to understand your needs, employ a disciplined approach, and have a strategy for helping you stay on track and accomplish your goals.

When it comes to getting started, you must first determine what success looks like for you. Then you must choose and build your portfolio. Finally, you must actively update your portfolio to make sure you stay on track.

DEFINING SUCCESS

As I discussed in a previous chapter, investing toward retirement begins with defining your objectives, which can be as simple as "I want to grow my money so that I have enough saved to live off my investments when I retire."

Maybe you already have enough—you've saved for years, and now you want your investment savings to generate even more income during retirement. As mentioned previously, you'll need to start by establishing your MRO, which means looking at the amount of return your investments need to generate to give you the lifestyle you want to live in retirement for the rest of your life (I know, I'm a broken record).

For instance, if you need an income of $100,000 in retirement, and expect around $30,000 from Social Security, and have another $30,000 from other sources such as a pension (for a total of $60,000), then your investments need to generate an additional $40,000 per year. Unless you have millions of dollars, a simple savings account will not return that $40,000 that you will need annually, and if you start eating into your principal you will more than likely outlive your savings.

The model we discussed already may be what you need to consider in order to live comfortably and confidently in those golden years. Again, what we recommend for many clients is the following asset allocation:

- 40 percent in stocks

- 10 percent in bonds

- 20 percent in REITs

- 10 percent in alternative strategies, such as options[*] contracts

- 20 percent in cash

This model, we find, has the potential to yield a 7 percent return or more annually in growth and income. Don't forget the model is not set in stone and needs to be managed proactively, depending on how your situation changes over time. While you're still working, you will probably have more in stocks and alternative strategies with potentially nothing in bonds. When you reach your later stages in life, where passing on your legacy becomes the goal, then you would have less in stocks and alternatives and more in bonds, REITs, and cash.

CHOOSE YOUR INVESTMENTS

Once you've defined your goals, established your MRO, and built a model based on our disciplined approach rules, then it's time choose investments to put in that model.

Start by looking at your current investments. If you are not retired already, many preretirees have money in a 401(k). The funds that you contribute to, that are hopefully matched by your employer, can and should be in the equivalent percentages to the asset allocation model we have decided was necessary for you to accomplish your saving's goals.

I can't help but to digress a bit at this point. If you have decided to manage your own money, one problem we continuously see when prospective clients bring us their statements is that they take on too much risk by overinvesting in too few individual funds or positions. Remember, as part of our disciplined approach, we never start an investment with more than 5 percent of the portfolio. Often, we'll

---

[*]   Only a very few of our clients have options in their portfolio and their use is limited to very specific individual client situations where their use may be appropriate.

even buy in smaller increments than 5 percent. For example, if Apple were a selected stock for our clients' portfolios, then applying the 5 percent rule to your $1 million portfolio, we would not invest more than $50,000 of the portfolio into Apple stock. It can grow beyond the 5 percent, but no more than 5 percent should be risked on any one investment position to start. Buy in with small increments. I live by this statement: "greedy pigs get slaughtered."

Another investing rule in our disciplined approach, as I've mentioned previously, is to never invest in anything that doesn't pay you for your time. Many people buy investments that don't pay them a dividend or interest while they're waiting for that investment to appreciate. Whatever you're buying—stocks, bonds, REITs, or options—should come with an adequate return on your investment in the form of a dividend, interest, or premium. If it does not come with an adequate return, then consider another investment.

> **I LIVE BY THIS STATEMENT: "GREEDY PIGS GET SLAUGHTERED."**

As I write this chapter, Apple is paying a dividend of 2 percent. Not great. However, Apple is one of the positions in our OneSource Health and Wealth Management Growth and Income portfolios that we also write weekly covered calls on (an alternative strategy). With those, currently, we're getting anywhere from fifty cents to one dollar per share in short option premium as an income on top of the 2 percent that Apple pays in a dividend. So, currently, I recommend that if you buy a stock such as Apple, you also look for additional income in the form of short (selling) options premiums. That can be pretty complicated for the everyday investor, so I recommend working with a money manager like my firm that is versed in strategies like covered call options or credit spreads with options to enhance your income. Again, the Apple example is a current example as I write this chapter, but remember to never fall in love with any one position or strategy. Be proactive; don't just put any old investment in your portfolio—and that's determined by your MRO, your lifestyle, and your needs. In essence, what return do you need to achieve your goals, and will the investment portfolio, such as the example in this chapter, accomplish your goals?

ACTIVELY UPDATE YOUR MODEL

Once you've determined your MRO, have a model that will help you reach those goals and then purchase investments that align with your goals and that model. Do you put it all away and never look back until retirement? No. Set-it-and-forget-it is a mistake too many people make. They think it's okay to come up with a model, decide on their investments, put their money in them, and then let the cards fall where they may. That's what many 401(k)s are designed to be—a passive approach that hopefully produces the returns over time to have the total dollars you need to retire. Don't leave it up to chance. Also, don't think you need to become a day trader either.

Your portfolio needs to be actively managed, and its success needs to be measured each year, or more often, to determine whether you are still on track toward your goal. It needs to be rebalanced at least annually—that's the only way to ensure it will truly help you reach your desired outcome in our experiences.

IT'S NEVER TOO LATE TO BEGIN

It doesn't take much to get started. If you haven't saved until now, or you haven't invested outside of the low-interest products offered by your local bank, it's not too late. To keep up with inflation at any level, remember TINA, or *there is no alternative*, to investing in stocks or stock-like investments if you're going to potentially meet your objectives in retirement. There are many people who can live off of ultralow rates of return, but as you know by now, this book is not written for those people.

If you are not one of those very wealthy people, maybe now more than ever it's time to consider investing more in stocks and other investments that can help you have the income or growth that you need to keep up with inflation. I highly suggest working with an advisor who is a fiduciary to help you get the returns that you now know you need to survive. Unless you have a huge pension, which most people don't these days, you're going to have to rely on Social Security, 401(k)s, and IRAs, and the monies that you've saved on your own for your retirement. And if that's the case, you know you can't rely on a 1 percent return on your nest egg to generate any sort of respectable growth or income that you can live on. You can't expect that kind of return to give you enough money to last the rest of your life in retirement, especially if the annual inflation rate exceeds 3 percent per year.

So part of getting started is simply realizing that it's not too late to make your minimum return to objective. But that's going to take more than just a savings account at your local bank. In my experience, most people need somewhere between 5 percent and 15 percent return to supplement their lifestyle in retirement. And it's not too late to get there, if you know what to do or if you reach out to the right advisor for help.

YOU DECIDE...

- It's not too late to get started.

- If all you have is money sitting in a bank account, earning less than 1 percent interest, you'll need more to get to your minimum return to objective.

- Your portfolio needs to be actively managed.

- Once you've determined your minimum return to objective, created a model that will help you reach those goals, and implemented that model, then you must revisit it at least each year to determine whether you are still on track.

- If investing in the various markets is something you've never done before, then it's a good idea to rely on an experienced firm or money manager, someone who will take the time to understand your needs, employ a disciplined approach, and have a strategy for helping you stay on track and accomplish your goals.

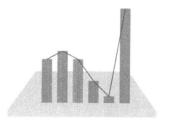

CONCLUSION

EXCITED, EDUCATED, AND EMPOWERED

W hen it comes to wealth management, I hope that the information in this book has helped you become *excited* about being a more active investor, *educated* in the basic yet powerful options available to you, and *empowered* by the realization that you can finally be on the right track to smarter, less volatile and rewarding investing.

To recap:

- You don't have to be wealthy to make substantial money on your money. You don't have to be satisfied with less in retirement or the status quo.

- There's more to investing than just what typical financial advisors in the banking world and big brokerage houses would have you believe is your best path to retirement. Why should someone with $500,000 to invest be satisfied with less than what the person with $5 million or $10 million expects in returns?

- The big investment firms are also banks. Their profits come before yours.

- Big investment brokerage firms have pay-to-play and preferred vendor lists. These firms are very expensive to operate, and they have to offset those costs, which is not in your best interests first.

- There is a better way than the typical "strategy" that big firms offer when it comes to taking your distribution or creating income when the time comes.

- There are two types of management when it comes to your portfolio—passive management and active management.

- Buy-and-hold forever is for suckers. Big institutions want you to keep buying more funds because they make more money off them; their own interests come first, then their shareholders, and then their clients.

- The market is two-way: whether it's real estate, a stock, a bond, or a car, there is a buyer and a seller in the transaction. On the other side of your trade is an institution or person betting against you, and your odds of winning are very low as a pure speculator.

- Don't pay for a written comprehensive financial plan that you throw away or never look at. A plan should be included in the fees you pay for investment management. The truth is most of the comprehensive plan that you may be paying for is pretty much common sense.

- Because of inflation, every day that your money is in a low-return account, you're losing money. Your low-return investments are not keeping pace with inflation increases.

- The masses have been taught that Wall Street is where the wealthy people are, and creating and having wealth is greedy. Main Street operates on too much emotion; you cannot let fear drive your investment strategy.

- Remember TINA—when it comes to inflation, *there is no alternative* to investing in stocks.

- Many products are originally sold with a commission tied to them, either paid by the client upfront or paid out to the advisor or the salesperson by the vendor and tied to a long-term surrender charge period.

- There's a difference between financial advisors and portfolio managers, and knowing that can make all the difference in your expected outcomes.

- Don't manage your own money without following some form of a disciplined approach such as the one I've taught you: always be paid for your time; never invest more than 5 percent of your portfolio in one position to start; be proactive not reactive; and never put more than 50 percent of your money into any one asset class. Finally, always have cash in your portfolio so that you can be a buyer when things go on sale.

The fact is that most people have not saved enough for retirement. But there is hope.

Your situation may not be as bleak as it seems. Especially right now, as I write this book, we're having one of the best investment and stock market years that we've seen in a long time. It's perhaps an unfortunate truth, but with uncertainty comes opportunity. And if your portfolio is managed correctly, there's growth and substantial income to be made in any given market on any size account. Whether you go at it alone, or you choose to work with the right people, you should never settle for the status

THE FACT IS THAT MOST PEOPLE HAVE NOT SAVED ENOUGH FOR RETIREMENT. BUT THERE IS HOPE.

quo. Whether you've accumulated $500,000 or $5 million, you should get paid for your time and earn an amount of money that helps you reach your goals. You should never settle for something less.

If you don't have the time, energy, or desires to manage your own money, then hire a professional. When you hire a professional portfolio manager to manage your money directly, you are hiring that person to make the decisions for you. So experience, skill set, credentials, and success rate count. As a portfolio manager, I've managed people's money through three market crashes and successfully helped them reach their goals. We've made hundreds of clients' lives easier, even during challenging times, such as the coronavirus pandemic.

Transparency is key. At my firm, there are no hidden fees. We don't get product commissions, so we are not incentivized to sell you specific products or things that you do not need. We only have your best interests at heart.

"Pretty good" is not good enough when it comes to investment returns—not for your portfolio, not for anyone's portfolio. I want you to have great returns—you should expect more, and you should get it. And that means being with a firm that doesn't settle for pretty good.

If you are tired of less-than-adequate results and service, reach out to us at OneSource Advisors, www.healthwealthadvisory.com, for a no-obligation consultation. Let us help you exceed your retirement dreams.

CPSIA information can be obtained
at www.ICGtesting.com
Printed in the USA
FSHW020154141221
86848FS

9 781642 252255